Dear Ghana,

I love you and I'm proud to be Ghanaian

This book is dedicated to you!

How to get ahead in Ghana

Preface ....P 4

Status Quo .... P 10

How to get ahead　　　　　　　　　　**P17**

Step 1 - Get rid of your demons .... P 18

Step 2 - Get your mind right....................... P 25

Step 3 - What is your value? .... P 30

Step 4 - Preparedness .... P 35

Step 5 - Apply yourself ....P 42

Step 6 - Keep focused .... P 48

Step 7 - Continuously evolve .... P 53

Step 8 - Be true to yourself .... P 58

Step 9 - It could be easy ....P 62

Step 10 - Dig deep, then even deeper......... P 67

Summary of Steps.................................... P 71

The Results　　　　　　　　　　　　**P74**

True Value defined .... P 75

Step ahead of the rest ....P 77

Opportunities in abundance .... P 81

Go get it! .... P 84

HOW TO GET AHEAD IN GHANA

Preface

In 2008, I experienced a spiritual calling to move to Ghana. I come from a family of four - my eldest siblings are half Ghanaian and half Lebanese, they were born in Ghana. My mother migrated to London, UK, met my father and gave birth to me. I identified as a Black British for the longest time because although my parents used to speak Twi & Ga at home and at family functions, and I would eat our food. I never could identify with being a Ghanaian. I couldn't understand why my family did certain things like 'pouring libation', I never understood the culture and most importantly I never understood why my aunties spoke so loud.

Fast forward 2008, my partner and I at the time, had a 2-4 year plan to move to Ghana to see what life would be like and to take advantage of the opportunities we heard of plus seek a better quality of life. That 2-year plan became 1 year as the week we made our plans was the week I found out I was pregnant! To provide context, our plans to come to Ghana was based on when we would be ready to start a family.

"Many are the plans in the mind of a man, but it is the purpose of the Lord that will stand."
Proverbs 19:21

Committed to the plan in 2009, I came to Ghana with my newborn and started my first business in 2010 with the will of God on my side.

After 9 years on the continent, I've seen and experienced recurring challenges when it comes to human resources. It appears that, we are busy chasing something which doesn't belong to us, we are in a rush, we don't see the opportunities, we blindly follow and for some, we get so caught up in somebody else's progress we spend energy in pulling others down. This translates into bad energy, eroded trust and weakens us as a nation, and ultimately a race.

I believe we need a revolution in terms of how we think, process and act and it starts at an individual, personal level - with you!
We all have a role to play, not everybody should be a business owner, not everybody should be a CEO, not everybody should be an influencer, a celebrity, an actor or a doctor! It's ok to be a cleaner, just be the best cleaner you can be. It is ok to be an office manager, just be the best office manager that you can be.

After mentoring many people over the years I've noticed many are walking blindly and cannot see the thin line they need to cross to get them from where they are now to where they need to be.

This book can be applied to any part of the world, not just Ghana, yet I wanted to be intentional and speak directly to Ghanaians for my first book because I believe our people need to read this and be empowered and start applying it today in their lives. There is something everybody needs to know and understand - there are no limitations other than what you place on yourself.

We are a new generation and this continent is for us! We define what our future looks, feels and sounds like so we need to start with our own why!

If you're not in Ghana or Ghanaian this book still applies because the principle is the same everywhere you go. If you're on the continent or in Asia, America's we have very similar cultural, religious and family myriads, so replace Ghana with your country name. In the West, I feel the environment is pre-fabricated with systems and rules which we fall into and are guided by. I believe this results in the free will being restricted and often suppressed by us in order to conform and survive.

People often find themselves in a marriage with children and working 9 to 5, only to feel unhappy, trapped and wanting more out of life. But debt and responsibilities and the fear of bad credit, keep people locked into the system. In my opinion, the trade of stable electricity, apparently better governance, democracy, good roads, safety et al is traded for one's independence, freedom, liberty, and true calling.

So in reading this book I pray - you wake up so you can say *'mannnn I'm done with this, I'm going to live my truest and best life'*. Once you empower yourself you will find it very liberating and you, in turn, will empower other people.

Returning to my journey to Ghana and living my why, by early 2008, I was working in a senior position within a media company, earning a high salary in the heart of London. I was 26 driving the latest Mercedes Benz Coupé, in a steady relationship and my boyfriend and I were living in a three-bedroom house with a big garden. I had by far passed a majority of my peers and I was knocking on a glass ceiling. I felt like all the checkboxes life had presented me had been ticked and I was asking what was next???

One Thursday I was being dropped off at West Ham tube station in East London, UK, and as I stepped out of the car, my spirit said 'You can't do this for the rest of your life!!!' I remember God speaking to me one evening telling me I had a Choice! He told me everything is my own choice so I should decide what choices I'm going to make for my life.

As I pondered on this revelation, the next thing that I heard was 'What's the worst that can happen?'. Every new or big life choice which came to mind -

my dreams - God kept on asking me 'What's the worst that can happen?', this continued until I decided to take a leap of faith - my first step.

The visions and dreams which kept on re-occurring I learned were for me, and that's how my journey continued. The journey looked like me excelling to my fullest potential with no employer limiting me. I did well in school, great at work and I always felt and knew I had much more to offer the world, I was struggling being confined. I needed to be free to explore and be relentless in my discovery. I was embarking on a journey where I started to discover who Nadia really is and I was excited by what I was capable of doing. I had done my time in full-time employment, I was ready to face the entrepreneur world!

My why for this book is because I wish and pray every day that people can experience liberation and live in purpose which is destined for them.

I believe in you!!!
I want you to discover the truth which lies within you and live your best life.
I want you to be able to take advantage of the opportunities which are available and to carpe diem!
I want to contribute to empowering our nation and letting people know that we are great, amazing and have something unique to offer this world!
I want to encourage you to go on your
journey, learn from the people you meet

and the experiences you have at every point, break traditions, boundaries, and perceptions and truly take charge of what belongs to you...your life!

I am not rich in money, I am not anywhere, where I want to be, but I am on the journey and at this point, I believe I have been called to share with you what I have experienced and learned so far for your empowerment - in order for your journey to commence and/or to be further refined.

Little drops eventually make a big ocean, so this is my contribution.

"It's the little things citizens do. That's what will make the difference." - Solome Nakaweesi Kimbugwe

The Status Quo

How the majority of people approach work and business

After 9 years of being on the continent and recruiting, training, promoting and firing staff, plus my interaction with people and those who are in a career - I've noticed a pattern, personal discipline is something which many struggle to implement, therefore when it comes to the workplace regulations and practices, people find it hard to respect and abide by them. I'm honestly beginning to believe 80% of the people who say they want to work, don't really want to work unless it is on their own terms.

Outside of the corporate world, I have come across numerous ways that people make money which helped me not take everything I saw in business and in life at face value.

Below I have featured different ways which I have heard and learned people make money in this country, however, to be honest, the modes of money-making I have listed can be applied <u>anywhere</u> around the world:

Entrepreneur Fever

Approx 98% of the people I come across want to be an entrepreneur, I want to run my own business they say - be my own boss they say! Be like you...some

say! I gaze and ask them - do you know what it takes
to be an entrepreneur?
I understand as a nation we rely
heavily on entrepreneurial activity,
but there are so many people who
are not cut out to be entrepreneurs. I guess a key
question is to ask yourself - what kind of entrepreneur
do you want to be? (Search online for the 7 different
types of entrepreneurs). Also, is your venture a means
to an end or something which you hope to nurture
and grow to stand the test of time.

Just that 1%

There is a perception that the big-ticket deals and
transactions are only operated amongst Ghana's 1%
- the elite crowd! Those that belong to certain politi-
cal parties and their cronies. Those that have had a
supposedly better quality education in foreign countries and are well-traveled. Apparently, the same
people get access to key individuals globally, walk-in
limited circles, fly first or business class or in private
jets, chill at exclusive parties and only share business
amongst their circles. Some of the 1% are accused of
stealing money from government coiffeurs and
Ghanaians as a whole - the claimed extent to the
shady deals are overwhelming - but as our court jus-
tice states 'innocent until proven guilty' and so it
goes...

The Hustlers

The objective of the hustler is money! It doesn't matter how the hustler makes his/her money, they just want to make it and live their life. The hustler generally doesn't mind dibble dabbling in some illegal matters or morally compromising activities, as long as they can achieve a quick turn around and make money. Hustlers often have three or more gigs going at a time, waiting on any one of them to payout. In the meantime, the hustler continues to look for opportunities that they can exploit. A quick transactional turnaround is always ideal with as few middlemen as possible.

Drugs

All that glitters isn't gold - word on the street is that we have a booming drug trade where we dabble in both import and export of illegal substances. This is no surprise, which part of the world doesn't? Ghana is popularly known on the streets of the US, Brazil, UK and many more countries for the referenced illegal trade. There are many people whose lifestyles are funded by the drug trade. People would see drug participants in society doing very well and aspire to have what they own without knowing what they are doing and most importantly what it takes.

Sugar Mama or Papa

Monogamy - an age-old argument suggesting that this ideology is a western construct. There is a strong belief Africans and/or the old world order/culture was structured around polygamy. People have quoted the bible where God's men were polygamists so why is it now frowned upon? The idea of polygamy was mainly based on the notion that a man would be wealthy enough to marry more than one woman and have many offspring. He would house them, feed them, spend his time equally with his wives and ensure all of his children go to school. Polygamy still occurs in some religions and cultures around the world, coexisting with 'infidelity'. Men are married to one woman and they have side chicks. The man still commits to looking after his side chick and giving her the things that she needs, but his wife just doesn't know about her - well, most of the time. Wealthy Women over the years have been picking up this trend with younger men - they provide for them as long as it is a mutually beneficial relationship.

Scrub/Pigeon

The over-entitled man/woman who behaves as though the world and everybody in it owes them something - they have an entitled mentality. The scrubs/pigeons of this world often don't have a job, they stay at home, dress up to go out and get other people to pay.

Juju - or something like that?

You've heard about them - Mallams, sakawa boys, human sacrifices and all of the juju activities that people are invest themselves in, to get money. I will leave this right here because I know some people are 50/50 about the idea of juju and whether it exists.

Money launders

Somebody said to me the other day - 'Nadia what exactly is money laundering?' Not because they didn't know what it meant but they contested whether it is illegal, and if it is, what constitutes it as such? Another person said to me 'Nadia rich people have got problems too, sometimes they have too much money they don't know what to do with it'. I hear this argument and understand sometimes global constructs tell us not to do something, which is being exploited by the very people who tell us not to do so. This can be frustrating for many, yet it is part of our status quo. Money launders often work on building a profile of themselves as a successful and wealthy entrepreneur living an elaborate lifestyle. This strategic move is to help market and position themselves to their target audience. Before you know it - they become kings and queens of industries.

They are recognized for their perceived success, pro-
filed by local and international media, they are fash-
ion-forward and are a public figure. The challenge is
society buys into their success and want to be like
them or want to follow them just by a
means of association, however they
don't scratch the surface to understand how that person got to where they are. The
truth of the matter 1+1 never equals 10 yet in the
world of money laundering, it almost certainly does.

The Grafters

The Grafters and the Hustlers have a very similar work
approach, it's just that with the grafters - they tend to
be 'straight down the line'. They are not interested in
anything which would compromise their integrity or
morals. They would rather labor and take the long
route to their own perceived success than to make
decisions that they will get exposed by or that they
will regret.

Our nation is full of grafters and we have many unsung heroes - when doing their work it often benefits
themselves, the people around them and generations to come. They tend to inspire people to be the
best that they can be! The grafters come in different
shapes and sizes - with different stories of their journey
and success. They understand the importance of personal growth and positively impacting others - they
are willing to do the long haul and although they as-

pire for the greatest things, they are comfortable with what they have.

**'Better is a poor man who walks in his integrity than a rich man who is crooked in his ways.'
Proverbs 28:6**

Action Point: *What category(s) do you fall in? Do you see your current lifestyle and work approach as sustainable? If not, what can you do differently or what can you do to improve?*

____

____

____

____

____

____

____

____

____

____

____

____

____

____

____

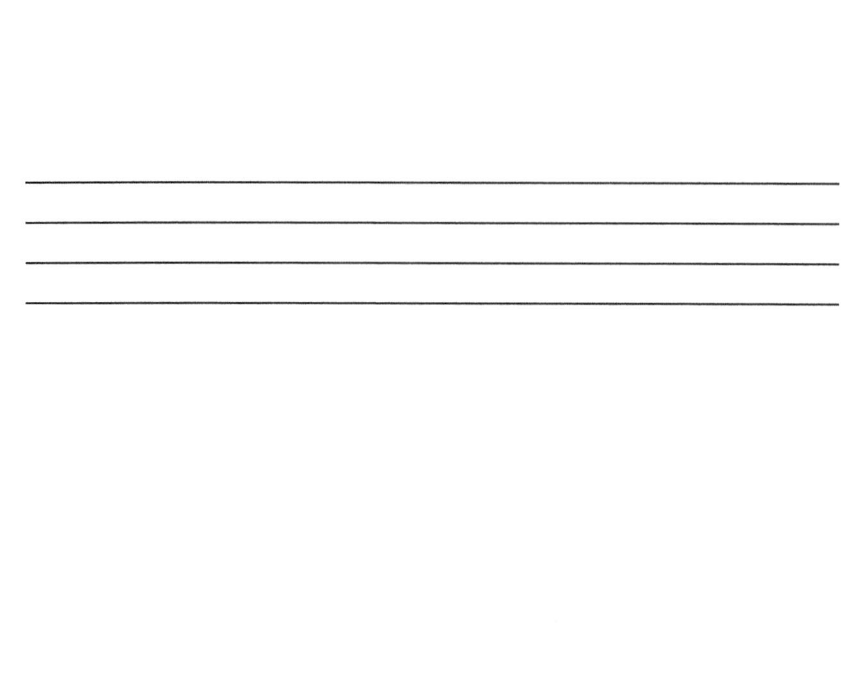

HOW
TO GET
AHEAD

"..a time to search and a time to give up,
a time to keep and a time to throw away"
Ecclesiastes 3:6

Step 1: Get rid of your demons

Daddy, Mummy, sibling problems, friend problems, betrayal, death, trauma, tragedy, divorce, miscarriage, poverty, sexual, racial, physical, drug, alcohol abuse, compromised health, incarceration - we have all gone through our pains in life. Unfortunately, as long as we continue to live we are not void of bad times and/or bad things happening to us. It doesn't matter if you are the nicest person with the best intentions - the truth is people are always going to do what is good for them and sometimes that might mean hurting you in the process.

Whether you're conscious of it, you do the same to other people - it may not be your intention, yet it doesn't stop the fact that bad things do happen and we each play a role at times.

What is important is that we face our demons and expel them from our lives - no if's, but's, suppressing, running away or acting it out but truly sitting ourselves down and being honest - emptying out what we battle with every day and just staring it in the face whilst choosing for them to no longer be our stronghold.

In life I have grown to understand people and the reasons for their actions a bit better - a person who riddles themselves with drugs and/or alcohol all the time is more often than not, trying to run away from their reality. People don't want to face the reality of what has passed in their daily life, so when they are intoxicated it's their form of escapism. Everything they do and say from there onwards becomes a consequence of the state they are in - so can you hold them responsible for their actions?

A man/woman who is physically abusive is often so because he/she has been subject to abuse at some point in his/her life and they truly do not know how else to deal with a situation. They remember their frustrations and anger when they were beaten, and when that feeling gets triggered they only respond the way they know-how.

Sometimes, we get ourselves tied into matters which have nothing to do with us and we fight other people's battles. Maybe your parents are divorced and you are angry with your mum because of the way she treated your dad. I know it is hard to say, but that is your mum and dad's business, not yours.

My brother/ sister - I tell you there is nothing better than letting it all go!
Let it go! First of all, whatever has happened to you cannot be undone and may not ever be resolved, you have to start healing so you can live your best life.

You CANNOT live your best life whilst walking around with a burden, because it will get inflamed at different stages of your life and you will respond
to the feeling and potentially destroy

friendship's, relationship's, your career, business, your children, wife, husband - anything which means something to you. Remember everybody has their pains and their story that they're dealing with.

I am not saying 'let go' as if it is easy but I am challenging you, dear loved one, to stop and hold yourself accountable and say I need to stop and be the best version of me. I need to let go and forgive all that has been done to me and focus on what is for me.

What is important is not to have an expectation of the other person, but knowing genuinely that you are letting go of what was and trading in for what is to come.

The best thing you can do is to learn from your experiences and see how you can handle the situation differently to protect yourself in the future.

But if you choose…

If you choose...

My brother and sister, If you choose...

To remain….

You will not get far!

There are many people who are rich but not happy - because there is no peace, no love, no joy and they feel lonely. There have been many quotes stating money doesn't bring you joy and the love of money is the root of all evil - this book isn't about you chasing money or making money - it is about you being on the right path that you have been called to.

Freedom - Joy - Peace, Love are all gifts of the spirit that we have. Once we are able to embrace them, it means no matter what is going on in our lives or around us, we can live our best lives. We can still smile, we can still be optimistic and trust and believe good things will come to us and it is for us. You may have no money but when you have freedom, joy, love, and peace you will realize that you are rich.

"But the fruit of the Spirit is love, joy, peace, for-bearance, kindness, goodness, faithfulness, gentleness, and self-control…" Galatians 5:22-23

I am not being religious, I am writing from experience, and sharing my truth!

Start freeing your demons!

Action Point: *Write out all of your issues, demons and ism's, It doesn't matter how big or little they are write out all of the things which have kidnapped you emotionally, mentally and physically.*
Once you have written them all down, look at them on the paper and either get

somebody to talk to or speak to God about everything you have written down. How it made you feel, how you understand things to be, confess whether you can get over it or what you want to do. Be brutally honest, don't protect yourself from the feeling.

As you talk extensively, you will start being able to breathe, as you unload all of the crap - then say 'God (or Universe), I release this unto you'. Individually forgive everybody who has done you wrong, call their name and let them go from your mental and emotional zone. You need to love yourself more than anything that has happened or that is happening to you.

Loving yourself more looks like letting go of everything which is hindering you.

Decide what you want to say to expel them out of your life.

____

____

____

____

____

____

____

____

____

____

"Do not be conformed to this world, but be transformed by the renewal of your mind, that by testing you may discern what is the will of God, what is good and acceptable and perfect." Romans 12:2

Step 2: Get your mind right

Who are you? What is your purpose? Why are you doing what you're doing? What are you thinking about?

Getting your mind right is THE first thing you need to do in order to be successful in life. Your why is what you need to define, it's your personal mission statement on why you are committed to what you are doing.

Multi-millionaire Oprah Winfrey, born in 1954 Mississippi, USA, often recalls her grandmother's desires for her to be the best house help with a nice family, 'Oprah Gail you better watch me now cause one day you gon' know how to do this yourself', her grandmother used to say.

By 32 - Oprah Winfrey was one of America's richest females owning her OWN television network. Oprah Winfrey had the odds stacked against her, she went through a childhood of racism, poverty and sexual abuse - nevertheless Oprah rose to her calling.

'I wanted to be a teacher. And to be known for inspiring my students to be more than they thought they could be. I never imagined it would be on TV' stated Oprah Winfrey.
I believe there's a calling for all of us. I know that every human being has value and purpose. The real

work of our lives is to become aware, and awakened, to answer our call.'

Understanding 'your why' may not come easy to you. Some may know it immediately, others may have buried it, others hide it away because family, friends and social ridicule, ignore or shut down their idea. Others may genuinely not be in tune with their why and may not even know where or how to start with their discovery.

But it's there for everybody, I always tell my staff, my today was very evident when I was young. I've always been passionate about how to make the world a better place, to bring peace, happiness, and experiences. My how was supported by my passion to write short and long stories, poem's, film scripts and more from when I was 6. I couldn't draw but I was great at drama and making things up - incredibly imaginative and creative - my sister would attest to this.

To help get your mind right do not focus on money or fame. Your calling may not be recognized on a large scale and you equally may not make a lot of money or be rich, but you will experience a wealth of richness in your life, within your soul and to the people in which you interact with. I know nobody wants to hear this but trust me, liberation and living your divine purpose in obedience is a beautiful feeling, everything else is a bonus.

Why are you studying for a degree in a particular subject? Why are you working in an industry which you are not interested in? Why are you getting a Masters? Why do you want to be an entrepreneur? Why are you buying that particular car? Why do you want your ministry to be very big?

When we find our answers are based on other people or monetary reasons, for example - I am buying this car because all of my peers have nice cars and I am the only one that doesn't. Or I am working this job because it is paying me a lot of money - then your divine purpose, your true calling is being lost, as you're focusing on what matters on the outside as opposed to discovering what is required from the inside.

One time during a spiritual revelation I remember I heard Pastor Myles Monroe on tv in South Africa. He said 'We should never chase money. Like an apple tree that bears good fruit, people will come to the apple tree and pay what it's worth. But you never see people looking for apples on a barren tree'.

Life doesn't owe you anything, whether you come from a family that didn't have, whether you've had a tough or traumatic upbringing, whether you've had the best upbringing and you're a trust fund baby! You have a responsibility on this earth, you need to understand, accept and embrace what It Is. It may be different to who you have become.

Action Point: *Take some time to figure out your why! Get a quiet place for 1 hour and take some time to dig deep and unravel what you're passionate about and why you want to do it, beyond the material gratifications. If you already know your why, write it down and expand what you see in your future.*

"Have I not commanded you? Be strong and courageous. Do not be frightened, and do not be dismayed, for the Lord your God is with you wherever you go." Joshua 1:9

Step 3: What is your value?

Every time I have an interview with potential employees I ask 'What is your value?' And they are jarred for a response. I often hear 'I'm a hard worker, I like working in a team, I can work on my own....etc, etc' it's boring and cliché and their claims are highly subjective not necessarily based on what their work experience.

When I ask, what is your value, I really want to know 'What's good?' What am I getting from you which is valuable, rare and which would be of use to our company in order to achieve its objectives?

For example, if you are applying for a job as a digital marketer and I say ok so what value will you come and add - I need you to be able to wow me. Provide me with a situation analysis that you have assessed from my company, my perceived competitors - where you can see important areas of growth and then how you would ensure you will take my digital team from A to B'. Following up with work examples, personal examples, presenting case studies and market trends will blow me away! It will tell me that you know your worth and value and what you can bring to the company. It tells me that when you start work you mean business and you are taking no prisoners. It makes me confident to send you to a meeting on your own and it also makes me confident that you can build and lead a team.

When it comes to your salary, you need to state your worth in line with what the industry pays and our company will be willing to pay - as we know what we are getting from you.

Too many people cannot and/or do not show or demonstrate any value when the opportunity is presented to them!

Stating your worth can be tricky, you need to understand what stage of your career you are in and what you equally want to get out of the employment you are about to endeavor. Every step in your career or business development needs to be intentional - you need to know why you are doing your job as it pertains to what you will get out of it. Again, because money is not enough. You may sit in a job and make a lot of money but then 2 years of your life is being wasted in a stagnant role which doesn't offer any prospects and stunts your growth. Your career and business life is a journey, be intentional at every step of the way so you successfully arrive at your destination.

I have no problem with stating my worth, sometimes it means work gets turned away but that is ok, I know how and when I'm willing to negotiate. The challenge of not stating your worth and just going with anything - you may feel people are taking advantage of you, your time and not respecting your work. Knowing your value doesn't stop at the monetary aspect - it looks at how you approach your work, availability, lines of communication, what you are willing to do and not do and how you want your client/employer to feel about your input.

If you are not sure what your value is - think about positive things people say about you and what it means to them. This usually highlights your value to them and potentially other people. You get a good feeling when you know your value and you want to keep on sharing it with others over and over again.

Malcolm X said 'If you don't stand for something, you will fall for anything'.

Action Point: *Write down what you think your value is, then ask a good friend or a mentor to challenge your statement to see whether it is cliché or if you're really onto something*

____

____

____

____

____

____

____

____

____

____

"Go to the ant, O sluggard; consider her ways, and be wise. Without having any chief, officer, or ruler, she prepares her bread in summer and gathers her food in harvest. How long will you lie there, O sluggard? When will you arise from your sleep? A little sleep, a little slumber, a little folding of the hands to rest..."
Proverbs 6:6-11

Step 4: Preparedness

I printed a sample of this book and said 'nooo, I forgot my favorite step - Preparedness'
I remember when I was having a conversation with a friend about challenges, of many people not being prepared.

You know those instances when you are waiting to pay for something in a shop by card and it's late in the day, then the shop assistant tells you - they need to plug and charge the POS in order to use it. Or when a restaurant is open and you ask them what they have on their menu and they tell you - let me go and ask the chef. It really irks me - because I can't help but wonder what they have been doing all this time whilst at work.

You come to work, to be prepared for a majority of situations, when a customer needs to order food or when a customer wants to pay a bill is definitely the basics. So when you fall short of this, it just bothers me to ask, 'so what have you been doing all this while?'

Prepare in the Oxford dictionary means - made ready for use or ready to do or deal with something.

Preparedness is much deeper than this - when you look up the definition of preparedness in the Oxford dictionary it reads 'a state of readiness, especially for war'

Wikipedia goes on to define preparedness 'refers to a very concrete research-based set of actions that are then as precautionary measures in the face of potential disasters. These actions can include both physical preparations and training for emergency action'.

This is the kind of energy and attitude I believe it requires in order to be a winner. From my experience of operating a business and being a mother and living in Ghana, I have learned that preparedness always keeps me going, more so than just being prepared. Preparedness allows one to take into consideration all possibilities and to put things in place to reduce the chances of things not going how you plan or require and/or falling apart.

In the past, I have experienced that my staff don't get prepared or practice preparedness and would often walk into a situation and panic resulting in us falling short of what we could have potentially delivered. There is nothing worse than having an awesome concept/idea and then it is not realized because somebody decided not to follow through on the plan or consider and execute preparedness.

The How?

If you know when you are going to work or into town, there is traffic at a certain junction - leave 30 minutes before your regular time.

If you know you have deadlines to meet and require other people's input, plan the work, set a deadline, communicate an earlier deadline to third parties and ensure you are constantly on top of everybody to get things done and ensure you can deliver - before time.

When you start a new week, know ahead of time what you want to achieve and plan your week accordingly. Write down your objectives for the week and key activities that need to happen in order for you to achieve them.

When you want to start a business, write a business and marketing plan, work on a cash flow forecast - let somebody vet it before you start investing your money into your business venture. Understand where you want to take your business - will you franchise it? do you want to sell it in the future? - if so when? will you want your business to go public and float shares on the stock market?

When you are organizing an event, design a checklist and risk assessment for all that could possibly go wrong and ensure there is a back-up plan just in case something doesn't work out how it was intended.

When you are going to an interview for a job or a pitch for a client - knowing about the company, the work and its leadership is important and part of you being prepared. It is not good enough to say, 'I never got a chance to read up on your company before coming' - it is never a good look.

Getting other people's buy-in is essential! Everybody who is part of your execution needs to understand the importance of their role and how they fit into the big picture. I have learned that regardless of how much you communicate to people, they may never appreciate your level of detail but, as you go along, you notice the weak links and quickly remove them before they become an infectious disease in your environment.

The idea is to never leave anything to chance and to be intentional about your actions.
I am sure you have heard or read the popular quote by Benjamin Franklin - ' If you fail to plan, you plan to fail'.

I live by this quote, I believe there are no truer words said when it comes to planning, being prepared and preparedness.

Being prepared is the difference between being in-tentional about your success and just existing, hoping for something good to happen to you.

I believe that when opportunities are presented to us, they come for one of three reasons - one - to get you ready for what is to come. Two - because you are ready to take advantage of the opportunity which has been presented to you. Three - for you to pass the opportunity onto somebody else.

I talk about preparedness and not prepared because we need to be intentional and strategic to ensure that we are ready for everything that we walk into and are able to think about all possible outcomes and how we would respond to it. Preparedness for me is deep thinking and approach to a situation, walking through it in my mind over and over again until I am satisfied with an outcome.

Where I think many people fall short is that they just want to arrive at a situation or just cannot be bothered to think through a situation and just rely on others to come through. I think this is the most wreckless approach to work and life. If failure can be prevented by us being a bit more intentional about what we are doing, then let us do so. But there is nothing worse than failing when it is avoidable.

Dear friend, be prepared and apply preparedness at all times for all occasions. It is the difference between winning and losing.

Action Point: *Assess your life right now and areas where you could apply preparedness.*
Breakdown each area and detail how you can be better prepared to get the best outcome out of the situation. Write down moments where you have been prepared or applied preparedness and how it positively impacted you.

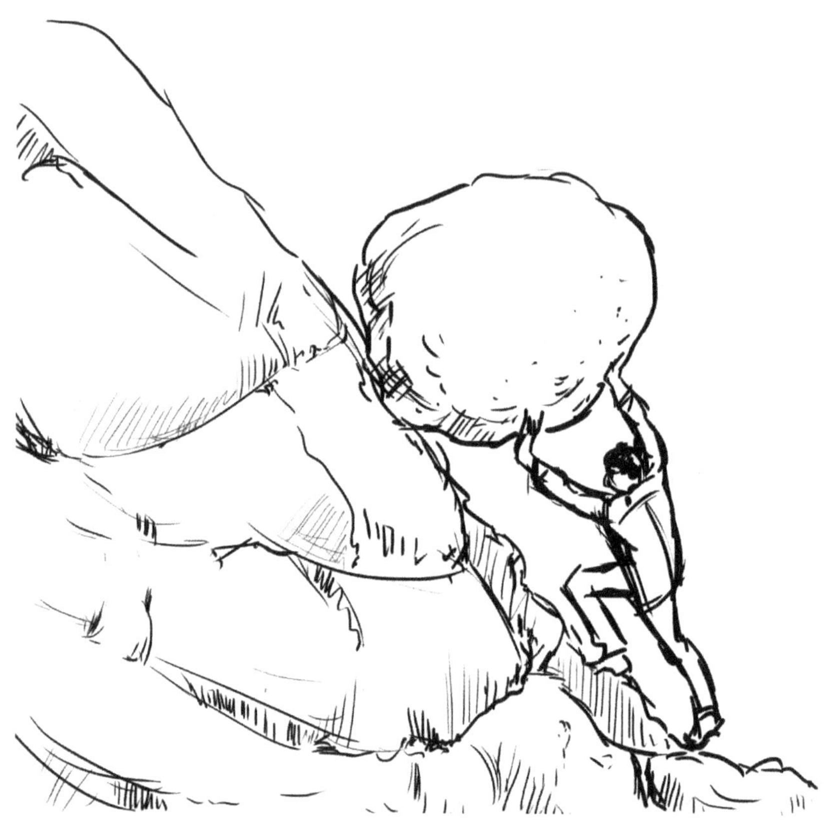

"Whatever you do, work at it with your whole being, for the Lord and not for men" Colossians 3:23

Step 5: Apply yourself

Running two SME businesses I've realized staff get very personal very quickly.
I tend to see the pride and ego kick in and then resentment towards me.
Some people have an attitude of 'hmmm you think you're somebody' followed by many contrived thoughts about how they are better than you and you're nothing.

I tend to see this behavior arise when one is constantly being corrected and begins to feel inadequate. That's never the intention but I've learned over the years that a lot of people like to be pampered and want to be given many chances. People often want to be told and/or fed work rather than independently thinking and applying themselves.

What many fail to realize is when you go and work for a company you are meant to do the work you have signed an agreement to do (your contract). You do the work and we will pay you. It is not work experience, it's not your family business or school, it is a place where two entities have come into a contractual agreement of works to be done.

When you start work, you need to respect and be disciplined to do your work and have the best interest of the company. Don't get into your head how much the company is making and the role you have in bringing in that money because honestly, that has nothing to do with you, you're not privy to the whole picture of how the business is being run.

What's important is that you deliver on what you are meant to do, to the best that you can and the company equally delivers in payment.

Work! Work and focus on God or if you're not spiritual focus on your purpose and not what your employer is or isn't doing. Have morals and respect yourself.

It's not nice if your employer has to ask you, why are you late? Why didn't you call? Why isn't the work done? Get off your phone! Why did you take so long for lunch? What kind of work is this? This doesn't look done at all!

It's equally frustrating to hear I'm sick, my family have asked me to travel to another town, I need to leave work to look after my brother's business, somebody in my family is dying, my phone battery died, going to a funeral, church et al - I know for some they are real reasons but too many people are using them to get off work for a day or two or five or to resign.

The constant interruptions to your work are exhausting and quickly ruins your reputation in the eyes of the employer/client.

You have to remember in every institution you are in, you want to leave on a good note and earn a reference providing confidence in the next company who wants to employ you. There is nothing worse than referrals being Pastors & Family members when you should have at least 2/3 strong references, from 2 years + work/voluntary experience.

Give work your 100% Everything you've got and what you didn't know you have! You will get tired of keeping up such great standards and that's because you may not be used to it - but when you keep on you will notice, applying yourself will become a habit and most importantly - respected!

80/20 Rule

The 80 / 20 rule is one of the most helpful concepts for life and time management, this rule suggests that 20 percent of your activities will account for 80 percent of your results.

What Is The 80/20 Rule?

The 80 / 20 rule is also called the *"Pareto Principle."* It was named after it's founder, the Italian economist Vilfredo Pareto, back in 1895. Pareto noticed that people in society seemed to divide naturally into what he called the *"vital few,"* or the top 20 percent in terms of money and influence, and the *"trivial many,"* or the bottom 80 percent.

Later, he discovered that virtually all economic activity was subject to this principle, in that 80 percent of the wealth of Italy during that time was controlled by 20 percent of the population.

You can take the 80/20 rule and apply it to almost any situation. Understanding the principle is essential to learning how to prioritize your tasks, days, weeks, and months.

Applying yourself means you are setting standards and defines you from the rest and places you on the level of a few!

Action Point: *Assess your present approach to work or your clients. How would you rate your present efforts and attitude? Write down how you think you can improve and put it into action. See if your employers/ clients attitude positively changes towards you and note down how you feel about the change of the discourse between you and the rest of your team*

____

____

____

____

____

____

____

____

____

"Keep your head up, your eyes straight ahead, and your focus fixed on what is in front of you. Let your eyes look directly forward, and your gaze be straight before you. Take care you don't stray from the straight path, the way of truth, and you will safely reach the end of your road. Do not veer off course to the right or the left; step away from evil, and leave it behind." Proverbs 4:25-27

Step 6: Keep focused

Our journey is long! Sometimes you may find yourself in the same situation for a while - 1, 3, 5 years - you need to continue to persevere and keep focused.

The biggest challenge in life is going against what the rest of the world says or what culture likes to dictate...

You should go to university
You should be married by 30
You should have children by 32
You should have your own house
You should be driving an executive car at your age
You should have another child by now

Sometimes when you are following your purpose and working on getting ahead, your life may not go as you thought or how society dictates it and you need to be ready and comfortable with that!

It's tough, you may yearn for an 'ordinary' life which your friends and family may be living, but if you believe in what you're doing, you've got to believe that when the time is right everything which belongs to you will come to pass.

I'm not saying your work or business should take precedence over your life. I'm saying keep focused on what is right for you and allow things to happen naturally.

When you're working, and things are going absolutely wrong, or people turn against you or slander you keep focused. Constantly do the right thing and keep focused - it shall pass -

When money is drying up and you can't see through to the end of the week - keep focused on the prize and meditate on an answer, it is ALWAYS going to be ok.

If somebody has bad-mouthed you at work or set you up, say a prayer, keep your peace and trust the process - it shall all surely work out to your favor. Fight a good fight and always remain focused.

Some people or some things may try to get you off track because they are not comfortable with themselves, they are intimidated by you, they don't understand you, they are jealous et al - just trust that it is part of the process.

Keep your peace and stay focused!

Sometimes you can be your own enemy - you're at work and you are on your mobile phone, or you're watching videos on youtube on your company desktop. Or you are sleeping when your boss isn't around. You like having conversations with your colleagues and flirting instead of working. You keep looking at what other people are doing and getting drawn into an unnecessary drama that doesn't concern you.

You flick through social media and WhatsApp your friends! You're running a side business that is interfering with your work for somebody else! You're closing early from work because of a church program that is taking place throughout the week. You want to see your boyfriend or girlfriend every evening by force.

Keeping focused is not only about the distractions which are presented to you by outsiders, but the noise and distractions you enter into. Once you start silencing the unnecessary noises you will find that you have more time and energy to focus on the things which truly matter and pay forward to your success.

Action Point: *Life can throw many distractions at us - our phones, social media, negative press, Netflix, overbearing girlfriends, dominating boyfriends, parents, noisy siblings. List out your present distractions whether at home, work or socially and brainstorm what you can do to reduce the noise.*

____

____

____

____

____

____

____

____

____

____

"When you are evolving to your higher self, the road seems lonely, but you are simply shedding energies that no longer match the frequency of your destiny" Unknown

Step 7: Continuously Evolve

There are six important things for living a successful and fulfilling life: never stop dreaming, never stop believing, never stop giving, never stop trying, never stop learning and most importantly never stop loving.

The beautiful thing about life is that you never fully arrive - your destination is reached when you take your last breath!

The world is constantly changing, new innovations are being launched - technology is a rapid game-changer, our environment is changing - generations are responding differently to politics and economics and so much more - you can never stop learning! Your value comes from adapting and understanding the world you live in and knowing where you are placed.

You need to remain relevant, and as time goes on you may become an icon of your time because you influenced a way of being or process that people are inspired by.

I remember my brother who is 10 years older than me, repelled computers when they first came out. He said he was done at learning how to use the typewriter and didn't feel the need to learn how a computer works, he was simply overwhelmed. Yet as time passed and technology got more advanced he had to surrender to the desktop in order for him to stay relevant for employment purposes.

"If you want to hide something from a black person - put it in a book"

This old adage has been said about black people after it was taken out of context from a speech Malcolm X gave - he was referring to the time when the slave masters would hide things from the slaves and because the slaves were illiterates and had not been to school, they could not read - that is the original context of the statement. Yet time has challenged this statement until today.

Many young people do not read enough of the right things. We are so institutionalized by education, that once we are done, many do not want to read another book. We want to take things at face value and base our thoughts and knowledge on what he said/ she said. Ghana's present literacy rate is at 76% of the population as of 2015 which is a gradual improvement from 57.9% in 2000.

We need to work on broadening our knowledge and comprehension base to ensure that we are able to comprehend and apply what we know - after all, knowledge is only potential power.

Many people only know how to use the basic software packages on Microsoft Office. Many people don't know what's going on in their country let alone the rest of the world. Many people don't write good English within their office job! My point is there are always opportunities to learn and grow.

The World Wide Web offers people accessible opportunities to grow and learn things from the rest of the world. Simply choosing to live in our own bubble limits growth and what we can offer the world.

"You are the salt of the earth. But if the salt loses its savor, how can it be made salty again? It is no longer good for anything, except to be thrown out and trampled by men" - Matthew 5:13

Action Point: *Think about what areas of your life you can top up on which will define you further in your role. What will it take for you to do and when?*

____

____

____

____

____

____

____

____

____

____

____

'You're not lying to me, you're lying to your-self'

Step 8: Be true to yourself

When I was a young girl and it was presumed that I was lying, my dad would always sigh and say 'Girl, you're not lying to me, you're only lying to yourself'- it was powerful.

Sometimes you think you can live with lies but I guarantee you it always catches up with you.

Guys, I know a lot of us have ended up in jobs, marriages, courses, 'ships as a consequence of us being told to, or thinking it was the best thing to do, but today I ask you to be bold enough and ask yourself 'am I being true to myself?'

Too many times I've come across 60+-year-olds who have regrets regarding things they only wish they were bold enough to do. The good news is, some of them spur the younger generation on being true to themselves.

You are your own person! You came into this world as you and nobody else! You owe it to yourself to be the best version of you and not try to imitate somebody else.

The power of being true to yourself releases the passion, creativity, power, peace, and ease in pursuing what is for you! You will come alive and have much to offer the world.

Importantly for those of you who have children, it is incredibly important for them to see you being the best and truest version of you, it sets a great example and encourages them to take life by the horns and make it work for themselves.

Our children watch us - how we respond to people and the world! Are you a slave to the world? Does your world take take take? Are you constantly tired? Are you intimidated? Do you feel you can't do something because of what other people say? Are you loud or aggressive just to get attention? Do you control life rather than life controlling you? Are you depressed? stressed?

The other day I was in the lift with my son and there were a husband, wife and a newborn baby also in the lift. I was lightly singing a praise song - we get outside and my son said 'That was embarrassing!'
I asked 'What was embarrassing?'
He responded 'You were singing in the lift and there were people there!'
I said 'You may be embarrassed because you don't have the confidence to do it, but I'm perfectly fine with myself and found nothing wrong with singing in other peoples presence'.

It may seem harsh, but I wanted my son to understand that he was projecting his own insecurity onto me and I needed to make him aware, so he would challenge what limitations he is placing on himself and how he is defining things which happen in this world.

Side note: Not everybody who purchased this book has got to this point! I'm sure 80% are tired of reading and it's requiring too much work on themselves. People want quick fixes which don't involve them doing much - so congratulations on reaching this point.

You're part of the 20% - I'm confident that it means you are serious about your way forward and being a step ahead of everybody else.

Action Point: *Are you true to yourself? Do you wear what you want to wear? Do you style your hair how you want it to be styled? Do you drink in secret? Dig deep and question whether you are being true to yourself at every point of your life. If not, write them down and see what you can do to free yourself from your own bondage.*

____

____

____

____

____

____

____

____

"For I know the plans I have for you," declares the LORD, "plans to prosper you and not to harm you, plans to give you hope and a future" - Jeremiah 29:11

Step 9: It could be easy

After 10 years of trusting God, I ask myself has it been easy? I honestly think the answer is no!

It's not easy to go against the status quo
It's not easy not knowing your when…
It's not easy making sacrifices that you would never have thought you had to make
It's not easy being in the minority
It's not easy to stand in faith
It's not easy to ignore the weird looks people give you when you share your vision
It's not easy to bare the backbiting
It's not easy not knowing when your next pay cheque is coming
It's not easy hearing people speak badly about you when it's not your character they're attesting to but their perception or experience of you at a moment in time
It's not easy trying to keep your business to yourself and people being determined to share it
It's not easy losing friends
It's not easy not having many friends
It's not easy not having money to buy food at times
It's not easy re-wiring your mindset
It's not easy going against the grain

It's easier to stay the way you've been programmed and get on with life, be free and just do you.

I remember a family friend said to me one day 'I know you're different but can you try to fit in small?'

I looked at him pensively and said 'Errr no!'

I often get employees asking 'Why are we doing things one way when everybody else is doing it another?' the point is you don't want to be like everybody else!!!! God has a unique blueprint for everything that is for Him and I plan to keep to it.

'Everybody' doesn't stand out, but Dangote does, Oprah Winfrey does, Joyce Meyer does, Dentaa does, Anita Erskine does, Burna boy does, Kofi Annan did, Kwame Nkrumah did, Nelson Mandela did, Obama did, Sarkodie does, Genevieve is (you don't know about her yet) - people who chose not to be like 'everybody else' stand out for good reasons.

I tell you nothing comes easy / it's a journey - you win some battles, you lose some, you're in the wilderness at times and sometimes you're at the top of a mountain - endurance is key!

Equipping and preparing yourself for the times of nothing and the times of things not being what you expected or people not responding to you how you hoped contributes to your journey. You need to be willing to go on this journey and not stop or turn back,

Take a rest every now and then - but just do not stop!

I'm a God-fearing person and I get through by constantly asking God for direction and trying to be patient for Him to guide me. The other day I heard, in a sermon, that God will either show you the destination or the journey but never both! I'm not sure if one is better than the other, but what I know is that my faith and trust in God have grown immensely and I constantly put my trust in Him as I grow.

The more responsibility I have I know I cannot lean on my own understanding and I need the right support to get me to the next level. It's not easy because when things are going well I've had a past of arrogance and ignorance kick in, then I messed up, or as I say - I took over the wheel and crashed the car - it took me some time to learn humility!

If you're spiritual, I know for many it's not easy hearing God speak or knowing His voice and this becomes quite jarring - but start somewhere because daddy is always speaking to us. We just need to believe, be still and listen.

It's not easy - but honestly, it's worth it!

Action Point: *Start with what small steps you can take today to start getting ahead! Don't overwhelm yourself and set yourself up for disappointment. Once you start you will feel accomplishment and you can build from there.*

"The purposes of a person's heart are deep waters, but one who has insight draws them out" - Proverbs 20:5

Step 10: Dig Deep, then even deeper!

One morning I was having a conversation with Daddy (as I call God). It was a profound conversation because I was telling him that I had not heard from him and asking if everything is ok. From here daddy, said to me that he wants our people to dig deeper. He told me too many of his children are living on the surface and he needs them to dig deeper to realize their potential and who they are.

He then showed me my body and he said 'People are working on their surface without wanting to start brushing off the debris and start to discover what they have to offer'. He went on further to tell me that some people do start scratching the surface and they think that they have found themselves and are whole.

Daddy then, showed me the earth - he told me just like an excavator needs to dig land in order to get to the real minerals and most natural resource, it is the same way we need to dig deep and find our true selves.

He then went on to show me how people find valuable resources in the land, they start digging and then they see evidence in the soil - they see evidence of gold, diamonds or some kind of natural resource. Then they invest in time, money and the right tools to be able to access what is beneath the soil.

Then here comes the big one daddy delivered to me - he said 'we are from the soil'!

"The Lord God formed a man from the dust of the earth" Genesis 2:7

So exactly, what we do in order to extract natural minerals and resources from the Earth is the same that we have to do to ourselves. POWERFUL!

We have the adequate tools to dig deep and get to our greatness yet we need to invest our time, be patient and persevere.

If we do not do so, we simply become an untapped resource!

Action Point: *Where are you on your journey of self-discovery? What are your crown jewels? How do you feel at this point in your life journey and how can you handle your self-realization better and/or differently in order to full press in?*

____

____

____

____

____

Summary of 10 Steps

So just to refresh on the step steps you need to take in order to get ahead.

Numero uno - Get rid of your demons, undertake an emotional health check and see where you are with things which have happened to you in life. If you realize that you are still bitter or you have matters which are unresolved, you have not let go of, undergo your healing journey today. Forgive and release all that you have hoarded in your heart and mind and set yourself free. Only then will you be able to commence your journey to greatness.

Numero 2 - Get your mind right - what is your why? Understand what is motivating you now and assess if you are in alignment with what you believe you feel inside. Adjust yourself accordingly and set your mind on the prize with no compromises. It is important that your spirit and mind are all aligned.

Numero 3 - What is your value? - what are your strengths which convert into tangible value for an employer or client? If you do not have any real strengths invest your time in both voluntary and internships in the absence of being employed. Discover your strength and build on it. Continue to read and study beyond what you see in

Ghana, and get a global perspective so you can broaden your potential scope and impact.

Numero 4 - Preparedness - this is beyond your standard being prepared. Work on being more intentional and strategic about your execution and safeguarding the work you want to achieve by taking a further step in being analytical and thorough with your work - creating a tight plan of action that has contingencies for anything which goes wrong.

Numero 5 - Apply yourself - give your best at everything, all of the time. Be your own barometer measuring your performance and contribution to your team and company. Don't think about who you are doing it for or the monetary value applied to it. Once you have decided to commit to something give 150%! No excuses! Omit as many distractions that you can and have fun along the way.

Numero 6 - Keep focused - Knowing why you are doing something, have your mind right and keep focused on the prize. Set in place what you want for yourself and ensure your actions are intended to lead you into what your purpose is. Keep your **eye on the prize.**

Numero 7 - Continuously evolve - don't stop learning and adjusting to the environment that you are in. Try and apply what you need in your life and remain competitive.

Numero 8 - Be true to yourself - Challenge yourself to do what you believe you are meant to be doing regardless of what society or your family tells you. Anything is possible when you are in alignment and working on purpose. Things fall into place and confirm your steps and actions. When you are true to yourself you feel happy, free, empowered and passionate about your everyday work.

Numero 9 - It could be easy - if the journey was easy then it wouldn't be worth it. We wouldn't learn what we need and grow in life to achieve some of the greater things we aspire to. We need to realise that being the best version of ourselves will come with its challenges, but we need to remain committed to our cause.

Numero 10 - Dig deep, then even deeper - continuously embark on self-discovery. Learn more about who you are, what you can do, what you have to offer to the people around you and the world. Respond to your spiritual direction and see where it takes you. Keep on digging deep to find your crown jewels.

THE
RESULTS

True value defined

'There's no passion to be found in playing small, in settling for a life that is less than the one you are capable of living' - Nelson Mandela

The most important takeaway from reading this book is that you are going to be a better person in pursuing this journey- no doubt 100% and there is no greater reward.

You will be a fig tree producing fruit, no longer barren!

You will feel confident from the core, you will know who you are and your worth. You shall be moulded in such a way that you choose your battles, you place yourself in certain spaces, you hold yourself up in a respectable manner and in turn you will be powerful!

People will notice you, admire you, some dislike you but still you would be a whole person constantly being refined.

Your transformation will change your attitude and outlook on life - fundamentally birthing a new you. Your relationship with your partner, friends, family, and colleagues will change.

Just like an apple tree, people will come to you for your fruit!

Your true value would be defined most importantly for you and the world will get to experience it.

Remember life is not a destination, it is a journey!

Step ahead of the rest

"No person is born great. Great people become great when others are sleeping" Nelson Mandela

Honestly, too many people are doing the same thing, making the same decisions and blindly following others or society. Taking action, applying everything you've read in this book will place you leaps and bounds ahead of your peers and present you as a viable, valuable option to employers, potential clients and more.

You've got to remember people are looking for individuals and organizations who can meet them at their place of need and support them, especially in our environment.

I remember a Malaysian client had come in from South Africa and they were looking for an office administrator/ manager. The company was offering GHC2,000 a month as a basic salary with benefits. They recruited a young lady who didn't know how to use Microsoft Word or Excel properly, she didn't have any project management or organization skills and lacked enthusiasm for the role - in hindsight I guess she was overwhelmed. Failing to rise to the opportunity presented to her, the young lady started checking out of her role and eventually started calling in sick at the time of their company launch.

I was sad for my client and ended up 'lending' them one of my staff until our contract expired. The company interviewed many candidates but the same challenge was always being presented - people didn't know how to package themselves and identify why they were suitable candidates for the role, I kept on telling myself at the time, 'Come on this is too easy!'.

These opportunities are low hanging fruit in our environment, businesses coming in from the outside want to work with people who actually 'get it'. This is one of their greatest challenges they have hence why they bring in a lot of expats and extend their employment and stay in Ghana. The transitioning from one country to another is challenging and can be the make or break of a company.

What I've noticed is that when people start seeing your value you quickly become high demand in this environment.

Over the years I have mentored and trained numerous staff and one thing which is consistent is that people find my working and management style challenging. Many have resigned and gone stark raging mad, threatening my well-being as they are infuriated about how they 'feel'.

Yet for me, what is important are those who perse-
vered -

One young lady landed a job at the British Council
after working at our establishment and for the past 6
years, she has risen in the ranks and is kicking ass.

Two ladies over the years, each started their own
events company, executing excellence and deliver-
ing amazing and memorable experiences to their
clients.

Another young lady has set up her own service business as and her partners identified a gap in the market which they believe their company can satisfy.

At some point over the years, each of them has re-
turned to our office and said 'Thank you' and testi-
fied that working with me was not easy but it was
definitely worth it, as now they are steps ahead of the
rest and doing what is true to them.

I am not attesting to 'making them', I am not saying
'if it wasn't for me, they wouldn't be where they are',
I am saying that I was part of their journey - and what
an honor it is.

I acknowledge my style isn't for everybody and I do
try to be inclusive and find a different approach for
people, however, I often find people are not willing to
meet me halfway which causes the biggest challenge.

If you want to be better, if you really want to be the best, be ready and put yourself forward all the time - regardless of how many times you get ignored or are told no!

Listen and learn from others who are in the know, gain experience from those who are doing something tangible.

'There is a time for everything, and a season for every activity under the heavens:' Ecclesiastes 3:1

Opportunities in abundance

"Do not discuss bread around birds ... do not discuss cheese with rats ... and for heaven's sake ... do not make moves or deals with snakes ... you have to be diligent at all times ... know your environment ... act and talk accordingly" - Fatima Alimohamed, African Brand Warrior

People often say the only way you can get ahead in Ghana is purely by who you know. Who you know helps but if you don't have anything to offer, who you know becomes highly irrelevant. The 'who you know' want to make sure that when they give you business or put you forward for a job that you're not going to embarrass them, only excel.

I encourage networking, upgrading your circles etc. but it's not the be-all and end-all. Being intentional about your career growth and development is critical to best position you for opportunities.

When people know you know your stuff they will become your brand ambassadors and speak about you in places you have not been before. They will refer you when people are asking for somebody in your profession. They will forward you emails when they see something that you could be interested in or benefit from.

They will nominate you for awards if they think you're an unsung hero in your industry! They will ask you for advice - people will approach you for interviews or provide opinions. People will know when it comes to your area of expertise then they need to come to you because you have substance.

The internet provides an opportunity for us to present more of ourselves and what we know online. So outside of the day to day interactions we can do podcasts, write blogs, record vlogs, share content and opinion pieces, create visual representations for your clients to engage in - constantly positioning yourself to your audience.

People from far and wide will start approaching you as they discover you and want to carry your wisdom to the world.

Your opportunities will come big and small - however when they come, always ensure as much as you can, that you control the narrative.

With interviews, you can ask to read the questions ahead of time and ask for a brief overview of what they are trying to achieve so you know how you can best provide content.

You may be invited to speak on a panel - get insight on the event and what the organizer wants to achieve by having you on the panel so you can plan and prepare yourself accordingly.

Always present an opportunity to
wow! Share and present material that
they may never have heard before. Take your audience on a journey with an experience that they will remember.

Keep in mind, it's not about the fame, it's about people having the opportunity to learn from you and you depositing seed into them so that they can potentially nurture and grow just like you are.

Go Get It!

"So I say to you: Ask and it will be given to you; seek and you will find; knock and the door will be opened to you. - Luke 11:19

There is nothing gained in sitting down overthinking things or waiting for something to be perfect!
I think perfection can be aspired to, and when we take actions it is realized.

Many people talk about the natural resources Africa has but there is one key thing they miss out - human resources.

I think we, as Africans are amazing people abound with a beautiful culture, a beautiful presence, and abundance in opportunity.

There is nothing out there which is better than where you are right now. Every country every continent bares their own cross and yet they make the best of where they are and what they have. It is down to us to make the best of where and who we are.

Invest in yourself - read, write, network, do something different - be kind!

Go on a journey of self-discovery, let go of pains, anger, disappointments and hurt because one thing I have learned in life is all of those negative energies only hinders your life.

Truly forgive, ask God to search your heart. You cannot bear good fruit with bad or contaminated soil. It won't take long until people start to experience your bitterness and avoid coming to you.

Don't be short-sighted! I see a lot of people who are doing well in their careers and business and they act 'too know' and before a matter of time their fall comes. Be humble in all situations and walk with grace and honour.

Avoid toxic things and behaviours in your life, it could be family, friends, gadgets, etc, identify them and remove it from your life as it will constantly hinder you as you pursue your journey.

I'm not 'there' yet! But I've seen and learned a lot on my journey so far - I don't think you need to be famous or rich before you share your journey to encourage others.

I'm on this journey and I'm saying, get up, dust yourself off and get on track - it may be better than what you're doing now.

If you start then stop - every minute presents you with an opportunity to start again. Learn your stride and walk your walk!

I don't want to stop writing but truly - go get it, your
life is for you...go get it!

"Knowledge is only potential power. It becomes
power only when, and if, it is organized into definite
plans of action, and directed to a definite end."
Napolean Hill

"You are the light of the world. A town built on a hill cannot be hidden" Matthew 5:14